A Woollytui
Christmas

Kerry Lucas

Beercott

Happy Knitting

Kerry Lucas

A Woollyful Christmas by Kerry Lucas

First Published in Great Britain in 2017 by Beercott Books.

ISBN 978-1-9997429-1-1

A catalogue record of this book is available from the British Library.

Typesetting, photography and extra technical content by Simon Lucas

Any errors found after publication will be published on our website at beercottbooks.co.uk/errata

www.facebook.com/craftykestrel
beercottboooks.co.uk
www.facebook.com/beercottbooks

Beercott

Contents

Introduction.

I love Christmas! And who doesn't? To me, Christmas means two things – family and fun!

In this book, I have put together a group of festive character knits which I hope will give you a lot of joy at Christmas. The patterns are all straight forward, and each character can be completed in just a few hours.

Accompanying Santa (or Nick Claus as I have called him), you will find adorable characters such as Pablo the Penguin and Simon the Snowman, as well as an elf, a fairy and of course a red-nosed reindeer. Great for sitting on a shelf or under the tree, I hope they bring little smiles of joy at this fun time of year.

Happy knitting!

Kerry

Materials and tools.

Most of the characters in this book are knitted using 3mm needles and double knitting weight yarn. To complete all the patterns in this book, including the clothes for the charcters, you will need the following materials:

3mm knitting needles
3mm double-ended knitting needles
4mm knitting needles
Stitch holders
Embroidery needle
Double knitting wool in various colours
6mm safety eyes
12mm safety eyes or buttons
Toy stuffing

Abbreviations:

k: knit
p: purl
inc-kw: increase knit-wise by knitting into the front and back of the same stitch
inc-pw: increase purl-wise by purling into the front and back of the same stitch
k2tog: knit 2 together
p2tog: purl 2 together
st: stitch
stst: stocking stitch - work alternate rows of knit and purl
(n): n number of stitches
(xxx) n times: repeat (xxx) n number of times

Pablo the Penguin

Materials.

To make Pablo you will need the following:

DK wool in white

DK wool in black

DK wool in yellow

DK wool in a colour of your choice for the scarf

2 x 6mm safety eyes

stuffing

3mm knitting needles

embroidery needle

Head.

Starting at the front of the head and leaving a long end, cast on 3 st using BLACK and 3mm needles

Row 1: (inc-kw) 3 times (6)
Row 2: purl
Row 3: (inc-kw) 6 times (12)
Row 4: purl
Row 5: (inc-kw, k2, inc-kw) 3 times (18)
Row 6: purl
Row 7: k5, inc-kw, k6 inc-kw, k5 (20)
Row 8: Purl
Row 9: K6, inc-kw, k6, inc-kw, k6 (22)
Row 10-16: starting and ending with a purl row, continue in stst
Row 17: (k2tog) 11 times (11)
Row 18: p2tog twice, p3, p2tog twice (7)

Break yarn leaving a long end for sewing up the head, and place the stitches on a stitch holder.

Belly

Starting at the bottom of the belly and leaving a long end, cast on 3 st using BLACK

Row 1: (inc-kw) 3 times (6)
Row 2: change to WHITE and purl
Row 3: k2, (inc-kw) twice, k2 (8)
Row 4: purl
Row 5: k2, inc-kw, k2, inc-kw, k2 (10)
Row 6: purl
Row 7: k2, inc-kw, k4, inc-kw, k2 (12)
Row 8: p2, inc-pw, p6, inc-pw, p2 (14)
Row 9: knit
Row 10: purl
Row 11: knit
Row 12: purl
Row 13: k2, k2tog, k6, k2tog, k2 (12)
Row 14: p2, p2tog, p4, p2tog, p2 (10)
Row 15: k2, k2tog, k2, k2tog, k2 (8)
Row 16: purl
Row 17: knit
Row 18: purl
Row 19: knit
Row 20: purl
Row 21: knit
Row 22: purl
Row 23: knit
Row 24: purl
Row 25: k1, (k2tog, k1) twice, k1 (6)
Row 26: purl
Row 27: change to BLACK, (k1, k2tog) twice (4)
Row 28: purl
Row 29: (k2tog) twice (2)
Row 30: cast-off kw.

Break off yarn leaving a long end.

Back

Starting at the bottom of the back and leaving a long end, cast on 5 st using BLACK

Row 1: (inc-kw) 5 times (10)
Row 2: purl
Row 3: (k1, inc-kw) 5 times (15)
Row 4: purl
Row 5: (k2, inc-kw, k2, inc-w) twice, k2, inc-kw (20)
Row 6: purl
Row 7-24: starting with a knit row, continue in stst
Row 25: (k2, k2tog) 4 times, k2tog, k2 (15)
Row 26: purl
Row 27: (k1, k2tog) 5 times (10)
Row 28: (p1, p2tog) 3 times, p1 (7)
Row 29: (k1, k2tog) twice, k1 (5)
Row 30: cast-off pw.

Break off yarn leaving a long end.

Beak

Using YELLOW and 3mm needles cast on 8 st

Row 1: knit
Row 2: k2tog, k4, k2tog (6)
Row 3: knit
Row 4: k2tog, k2, k2tog (4)
Row 5: knit
Row 6: (k2tog) twice (2)
Row 7: k2tog

Fasten off the yarn leaving an end to sew beak together.

Wings (Make 2)

Using BLACK and 3mm needles cast on 3 st.

Row 1: inc-kw, k2 (4)
Row 2: knit
Row 3: inc-kw, k3 (5)
Row 4-9: knit
Row 10: inc-kw, k4 (6)
Row 11-16: knit
Row 17: inc-kw, k5 (7)
Row 18: k6, inc-kw (8)
Row 19: inc-kw, k7 (9)
Row 20: k8, inc-kw (10)
Row 21: inc-kw, k9 (11)
Row 22: knit
Row 23: k2tog, k7, k2tog (9)
Row 24: k2tog, k5, k2tog (7)
Row 25: k2tog, k3, k2tog (5)
Row 26: k2tog, k1, k2tog (3)

Cast off kw. Break yarn leaving an end for sewing the wing to the body.

Feet

Cast on 5 st using YELLOW and 3mm needles

Row 1: k5
Row 2: k5
Row 3: k1, p1, k1, p1, k1
Row 4: p1, inc-kw, p1, inc-kw, p1 (7)
Row 5: k1, p2, k1, p2, k1
Row 6: p1, k1, inc-kw, p1, inc-kw, k1, p1 (9)
Row 7: k1, p3, k1, p3, k1
Row 8: p1, k1, inc-kw, k1, p1, k1, inc-kw, k1, p1 (11)
Row 9: k1, p4, k1, p4, k1
Row 10: p1, inc-kw, k1, inc-kw, k1, p1, k1, inc-kw, k1, inc-kw, p1 (15)
Row 11: k1, p6, k1, p6, k1
Row 12: cast-off 1 pw, cast-off 6 kw, cast-off 1 pw, cast-off 6-kw, cast-off 1 pw

Scarf

Using your chosen colour cast on 10 st using 3mm needles

Row 1: k2, p2, k2, p2, k2
Row 2: p2, k2, p2, k2, p2

repeat these two rows until the scarf measures approximately 210mm long.

Cast-off 2 kw, cast-off 2 pw etc. to end.

To make up

Head

Fit the safety eyes roughly half way along the head, and approximately a quarter of the width in from the edge. Thread the yarn from the last row of the head through the stitches remaining on the needle and pull tight, then remove the stitches from the needle. With right-sides together, sew along the underside of the head, leaving a small gap at the nose for stuffing. Turn the head the right way out, and stuff to the required firmness. Sew together the remaining opening and feed the end of the yarn back through the head before cutting off. Feed the remaining end back through the head before cutting off.

Body

With right sides together, sew the belly to the back down each side. Run a thread round the neck using a running stitch and gather, then fasten off.
Turn the body right-side out and stuff.
Sew up the bottom opening.

Thread the remaining end back up through the body before cutting off.

Beak

Fold the beak in half, and sew together along the edge to form a triangle, leaving the cast-on edge open. Feed the thread back through the beak before trimming.

Assembly:

Attach the head to the body, making sure the nose points forward.

Sew the beak to the front of the head, adding a little stuffing if desired.

Using the free thread, sew the wings to the sides of the body in the position shown.

Using the free thread, attach the feet to the underside of the body.

Simon the Snowman

Materials.

To make Simon you will need the following:

DK wool in white

DK wool in black

DK wool in orange

DK wool in a colour of your choice for the scarf

DK wool in colours a and b for the hat

2 x 6mm safety eyes

2 x 12mm black safety eyes or 2 black buttons

stuffing

3mm knitting needles

3mm double ended needles

4mm knitting needles

embroidery needle

Head

Starting at base, cast on 6 st in WHITE

Row 1: (inc-kw) 6 times (12)
Row 2: purl
Row 3: (k1, inc-kw) 6 times (18)
Row 4: purl
Row 5: (k2, inc-kw) 6 times (24)
Row 6: purl
Row 7: (k3, inc-kw) 6 times (30)
Row 8: purl
Row 9: knit
Row 10: purl
Row 11: (k3, k2tog) 6 times (24)
Row 12: purl
Row 13: (k2, k2tog) 6 times (18)
Row 14: purl
Row 15: (k1, k2tog) 6 times (12)

Row 16: purl
Row 17: (k2tog) 6 times (6)

Break off yarn leaving a long end and transfer to a stitch holder.

Body

Starting at bottom Cast on 6 st in WHITE

Row 1: (inc-kw) 6 times (12)
Row 2: purl
Row 3: (k1, inc-kw) 6 times (18)
Row 4: purl
Row 5: (k2, inc-kw) 6 times (24)
Row 6: purl
Row 7: (k3, inc-kw) 6 times (30)
Row 8: purl
Row 9: (k4, inc-kw) 6 times (36)
Row 10: purl
Row 11: (k5, inc-kw) 6 times (42)
Row 12-18: continue in stst starting and ending with a purl row.
Row 19: (k5, k2tog) 6 times (36)
Row 20: purl
Row 21: (k4, k2tog) 6 times (30)
Row 22: purl
Row 23: (k3, k2tog) 6 times (24)
Row 24: purl
Row 25: (k2, k2tog) 6 times (18)
Row 26: purl
Row 27: (k1, k2tog) 6 times (12)
Row 28: purl
Row 29: (k2tog) 6 times (6)

Break off yarn leaving a long end and transfer to a stitch holder.

Arms (make 2)

Using 3mm double-ended needles and leaving a long end, cast on 3 st using WHITE and work i-cord as follows

Row 1: k3
Row 2: without turning the work, move the stitches to the other end of the needle, pass the wool round the back of the work. Keeping yarn tight, k3
Repeat row 2 until the arm measures 85mm.

Break off yarn leaving a long end, and transfer stitches to a stitch holder.

Legs (make 2)

Using 3mm double-ended needles and leaving a long end, cast on 4 st using WHITE and work i-cord as follows

Row 1: k4
Row 2: without turning the work, move the stitches to the other end of the needle, pass the wool round the back of the work. Keeping yarn tight, k4
Repeat row 2 until the leg measures 95mm.

Break off yarn leaving a long end, and transfer stitches to a stitch holder

Nose

Using ORANGE and 3mm needles cast on 8 st

Row 1-3: knit

Row 4: k2tog, k4, k2tog (6)
Row 5: knit
Row 6: k2tog, k2, k2tog (4)
Row 7: knit
Row 8: (k2tog) twice (2)
Row 9: k2tog

Fasten off the yarn leaving an end to sew nose together.

Boots (make 2)

Using BLACK and 4mm needles cast on 14 st

Row 1-2: knit
Row 3: K3, (K2tog) 4 times, K3 (10)
Row 4: K3, (K2tog) twice, K3 (8)
Row 5-6: knit
Cast-off knit-wise.

Break off yarn leaving a long end.

Scarf

using 3mm needles and your chosen colour cast on 5st

Row 1: k1, p1, k1, p1, k1

Repeat row 1 until the scarf reaches the required length (I find approximately 210mm looks good).

Cast-off kw then sew in ends before trimming.

Hat

Using WHITE and 3mm needles cast on 24st

Rows 1-4: (k2, p2) 12 times
Rows 5-14: change to colour a and continue in stst starting with a knit row and working 2 rows at a time of colours a and b alternately
Row 15: change to colour a, (k2tog) 12 times (12)
Row 16: (p2tog) 6 times (3)

To make up

Head

Fit the safety eyes roughly in the middle of the head, and close together. Thread the yarn from the last row of the head through the stitches remaining on the needle and pull tight, then remove the stitches from the needle. With right-sides together, sew along the back of the head, leaving a small gap at the base for stuffing. Turn the head the right way out, and stuff to the required firmness. Sew together the remaining opening and feed the end of the yarn back through the head before cutting off. Feed the remaining end back through the head before cutting off.

Body

Fit the 12mm safety eyes or buttons to the front of the body, evenly spaced apart as shown in the picture. Thread the yarn from the last row of the body through the stitches remaining on the needle and pull tight, then remove the stitches from the needle. With right-sides together, sew along the back of the body, leaving a small gap at the bottom for stuffing. Turn the body the right way out, and stuff to the required firmness. Sew together the remaining opening and feed the end of the yarn back through the body before cutting off. Feed the remaining end back through the body before cutting off.

Boots

Fold the boot in half and stitch down the back and along the bottom of the boot.

Arms

Thread the yarn from the last row of the arm through the stitches remaining on the needle and pull tight, then remove the stitches from the needle. Fasten off this end securely. Weave the other loose end up through the arm and cut off the excess.

Legs

Thread the yarn from the last row of the leg through the stitches remaining on the needle and pull tight, then remove the stitches from the needle. Fasten off this end securely. Weave the other loose end up through the leg and cut off the excess.

Hat

Thread the yarn from the last row of the hat through the stitches remaining on the needle and pull tight, then remove the stitches from the needle. With right-sides together, sew along the back of the hat. Feed the remaining end back through the hat before cutting off.

Nose

Fold the nose in half, and sew together along the edge to form a triangle, leaving the cast-on edge open. Feed the thread back through the nose before trimming.

Assembly:

Attach the head to the body, making sure the eyes point forward (the body seam should be at the back).

Sew the nose to the front of the head between and just below the eyes, adding a little stuffing if desired.

Using the free thread, attach the arms to the body just below the head, one on each side.

Using the free thread, attach the legs to the underside of the body.

Feed the each leg into a boot and fasten with a small stitch.

Nick Claus (Santa)

Materials.

To make Nick you will need the following:

DK wool in white

DK wool in black

DK wool in pink

DK wool in red

2 x 6mm safety eyes

stuffing

3mm knitting needles

3mm double ended needles

4mm knitting needles

embroidery needle

Head

Starting at base, cast on 6 st in PINK

Row 1: (inc-kw) 6 times (12)
Row 2: purl
Row 3: (k1, inc-kw) 6 times (18)
Row 4: purl
Row 5: (k2, inc-kw) 6 times (24)
Row 6: purl
Row 7: (k3, inc-kw) 6 times (30)
Row 8: purl
Row 9: knit
Row 10: purl
Row 11: (k3, k2tog) 6 times (24)
Row 12: purl
Row 13: (k2, k2tog) 6 times (18)
Row 14: purl
Row 15: (k1, k2tog) 6 times (12)
Row 16: purl
Row 17: (k2tog) 6 times (6)

Break off yarn leaving a long end and transfer to a stitch holder.

Body.

Starting at the base of the body cast on 6 st in RED

Row 1: (inc-kw) 6 times (12)
Row 2: purl
Row 3: (k1, inc-kw) 6 times (18)
Row 4: purl
Row 5: (k2, inc-kw) 6 times (24)
Row 6: purl
Row 7: k10, inc-kw, k2, inc-kw, k10 (26)
Row 8: p10, inc-pw, p1, inc-pw twice, p1, inc-pw, p10 (30)
Row 9: k10, inc-kw, k1, inc-kw, k4, inc-kw, k1, inc-kw, k10 (34)
Row 10: purl
Row 11: knit
Row 12: purl
Row 13: k10, k2tog, k1, k2tog, k4, k2tog, k1, k2tog, k10 (30)
Row 14: p10, p2tog, p1, p2tog twice, p1, p2tog, p10 (26)
Row 15: k10, k2tog, k2, k2tog, k10 (24)
Row 16-19: change to BLACK and continue in stst starting with a purl row
Row 20-26: change to RED and continue in stst starting and ending with a purl row
Row 27: (k2, k2tog) 6 times (18)
Row 28: purl
Row 29: (k1, k2tog) 6 times (12)
Row 30: purl
Row 31: (k2tog) 6 times (6)

Break off yarn leaving a long end to sew up body, and transfer stitches to a stitch holder.

Arms (make 2)

Using 3mm double-ended needles and leaving a long end, cast on 3 st using RED and work i-cord as follows

Row 1: k3
Row 2: without turning the work, move the stitches to the other end of the needle, pass the wool round the back of the work. Keeping yarn tight, k3
Repeat row 2 until the arm measures 85mm.

Break off yarn leaving a long end, and transfer stitches to a stitch holder.

Legs (make 2)

Using 3mm double-ended needles and leaving a long end, cast on 4 st using RED and work i-cord as follows

Row 1: k4
Row 2: without turning the work, move the stitches to the other end of the needle, pass the wool round the back of the work. Keeping yarn tight, k4
Repeat row 2 until the leg measures 95mm.

Break off yarn leaving a long end, and transfer stitches to a stitch holder

Boots (make 2)

Using BLACK and 4mm needles cast on 14 st

Row 1-2: knit
Row 3: K3, (K2tog) 4 times, K3 (10)

Row 4: K3, (K2tog) twice, K3 (8)
Row 5-6: knit
Cast-off knit-wise.

Break off yarn leaving a long end.

Beard

Using WHITE cast on 10 st

Row 1: knit
Row 2: k2tog, k6, k2tog (8)
Row 3: knit
Row 4: k2tog, k4, k2tog (6)
Row 5: knit
Row 6: k2tog, k1, k2tog (4)
Row 7: knit
Row 8: (k2tog) twice (2)
Row 9: k2tog (1)

Break off yarn and fasten off.

Hat

using WHITE cast on 26 st

Row 1-4: purl
Row 5-16: change to RED and continue in stst, starting with a knit row
Row 17: (k2tog) 13 times (13)
Row 18: (k2tog) 6 times, k1 (7)

Break off yarn leaving a long end, and transfer stitches to a stitch holder

To make up

Head

Fit the safety eyes roughly in the middle of the head, and close together. Thread the yarn from the last row of the head through the stitches remaining on the needle and pull tight, then remove the stitches from the needle. With right-sides together, sew along the back of the head, leaving a small gap at the base for stuffing. Turn the head the right way out, and stuff to the required firmness. Sew together the remaining opening and feed the end of the yarn back through the head before cutting off. Feed the remaining end back through the head before cutting off.

Body

Thread the yarn from the last row of the body through the stitches remaining on the needle and pull tight, then remove the stitches from the needle. With right-sides together, sew along the back of the body, leaving a small gap at the bottom for stuffing. Turn the body the right way out, and stuff to the required firmness. Sew together the remaining opening and feed the end of the yarn back through the body before cutting off. Feed the remaining end back through the body before cutting off.

Boots

Fold the boot in half and stitch down the back and along the bottom of the boot.

Arms

Thread the yarn from the last row of the arm through the stitches remaining on the needle and pull tight, then remove the stitches from the needle. Fasten off this end securely. Weave the other loose end up through the arm and cut off the excess.

Legs

Thread the yarn from the last row of the leg through the stitches remaining on the needle and pull tight, then remove the stitches from the needle. Fasten off this end securely. Weave the other loose end up through the leg and cut off the excess.

Hat

Thread the yarn from the last row of the hat through the stitches remaining on the needle and pull tight, then remove the stitches from the needle. With right-sides together, sew along the back of the hat. Feed the remaining end back through the hat before cutting off.

Assembly:

Attach the head to the body, making sure the eyes point forward (the body seam should be at the back).

Sew the beard to the front of the just below the eyes.

Using the free thread, attach the arms to the body just below the head, one on each side.

Using the free thread, attach the legs to the underside of the body.

Feed the each leg into a boot and fasten with a small stitch.

Eric the Elf

Materials.

To make Eric you will need the following:

DK wool in white

DK wool in black

DK wool in pink

DK in your choice of colour for the body, arms and legs (main)

2 x 6mm safety eyes

stuffing

3mm knitting needles

3mm double ended needles

4mm knitting needles

embroidery needle

Head

Starting at base, cast on 6 st in PINK

Row 1: (inc-kw) 6 times (12)
Row 2: purl
Row 3: (k1, inc-kw) 6 times (18)
Row 4: purl
Row 5: (k2, inc-kw) 6 times (24)
Row 6: purl
Row 7: (k3, inc-kw) 6 times (30)
Row 8: purl
Row 9: knit
Row 10: purl
Row 11: (k3, k2tog) 6 times (24)
Row 12: purl
Row 13: (k2, k2tog) 6 times (18)
Row 14: purl
Row 15: (k1, k2tog) 6 times (12)
Row 16: purl

Row 17: (k2tog) 6 times (6)

Break off yarn leaving a long end and transfer to a stitch holder.

Body

Starting at the base of the body, cast on 6 st in MAIN

Row 1: (inc-kw) 6 times (12)
Row 2: purl
Row 3: (k1, inc-kw) 6 times (18)
Row 4: purl
Row 5: (k2, inc-kw) 6 times (24)
Row 6-11: starting with a purl row, continue in stst
Row 12-15: change to BLACK and continue in stst starting with a purl row
Row 16-30: change to MAIN and continue in stst, starting and ending with a purl row
Row 31: (k2, k2tog) 6 times (18)
Row 32: change to WHITE, purl
Row 33: (k1, k2tog) 6 times (12)
Row 34: purl
Row 35: (k2tog) 6 times (6)

Break off yarn leaving a long end and transfer stitches to a stitch holder.

Arms (make 2)

Using 3mm double-ended needles and leaving a long end, cast on 3 st using MAIN and work i-cord as follows

Row 1: k3

Row 2: without turning the work, move the stitches to the other end of the needle, pass the wool round the back of the work. Keeping yarn tight, k3
Repeat row 2 until the arm measures 85mm.

Break off yarn leaving a long end, and transfer stitches to a stitch holder.

Legs (make 2)

Using 3mm double-ended needles and leaving a long end, cast on 4 st using MAIN and work i-cord as follows

Row 1: k4
Row 2: without turning the work, move the stitches to the other end of the needle, pass the wool round the back of the work. Keeping yarn tight, k4
Repeat row 2 until the leg measures 95mm.

Break off yarn leaving a long end, and transfer stitches to a stitch holder

Hat

Using WHITE cast on 26 st

Row 1-4: purl
Row 5-16: change to MAIN and continue in stst, starting with a knit row
Row 17: k1, (k2tog, k1) 8 times, k1 (18)
Row 18: purl
Row 19: (k2tog, k1) 6 times (12)
Row 20: purl

Row 21: (k2tog) 6 times (6)
Row 22: Purl
Row 23: (k2tog) 3 times (3)

Break off yarn leaving a long end, and transfer stitches to a stitch holder

Boots (make 2)

Using WHITE and 4mm needles cast on 14 st

Row 1-2: knit
Row 3: K3, (K2tog) 4 times, K3 (10)
Row 4: K3, (K2tog) twice, K3 (8)
Row 5-6: knit
Cast-off knit-wise.

Break off yarn leaving a long end.

To make up

Head

Fit the safety eyes roughly in the middle of the head, and close together. Thread the yarn from the last row of the head through the stitches remaining on the needle and pull tight, then remove the stitches from the needle. With right-sides together, sew along the back of the head, leaving a small gap at the base for stuffing. Turn the head the right way out, and stuff to the required firmness. Sew together the remaining opening and feed the end of the yarn back through the head before cutting off. Feed the remaining end back through the head before cutting off.

Body

Thread the yarn from the last row of the body through the stitches remaining on the needle and pull tight, then remove the stitches from the needle. With right-sides together, sew along the back of the body, leaving a small gap at the bottom for stuffing. Turn the body the right way out, and stuff to the required firmness. Sew together the remaining opening and feed the end of the yarn back through the body before cutting off. Feed the remaining end back through the body before cutting off.

Arms

Thread the yarn from the last row of the arm through the stitches remaining on the needle and pull tight, then remove the stitches from the needle. Fasten off this end securely. Weave the other loose end up through the arm and cut off the excess.

Legs

Thread the yarn from the last row of the leg through the stitches remaining on the needle and pull tight, then remove the stitches from the needle. Fasten off this end securely. Weave the other loose end up through the leg and cut off the excess.

Hat

Thread the yarn from the last row of the hat through the stitches remaining on the needle and pull tight, then remove the stitches from the needle. With right-sides together, sew along the back of the hat. Feed the remaining end back through the hat before cutting off.

Boots

Fold the boot in half and stitch down the back and along the bottom of the boot.

Assembly:

Attach the head to the body, making sure the eyes point forward (the body seam should be at the back).

Using the free thread, attach the arms to the body just below the head, one on each side.

Using the free thread, attach the legs to the underside of the body.

Feed the each leg into a boot and fasten with a small stitch.

Flo the Fairy

Materials.

To make Flo you will need the following:

DK wool in white

DK wool in your choice of hair colour

DK wool in pink

DK in your choice of colour for the body (main)

2 x 6mm safety eyes

stuffing

3mm knitting needles

3mm double ended needles

embroidery needle

Head

Starting at base, cast on 6 st in PINK

Row 1: (inc-kw) 6 times (12)
Row 2: purl
Row 3: (k1, inc-kw) 6 times (18)
Row 4: purl
Row 5: (k2, inc-kw) 6 times (24)
Row 6: purl
Row 7: (k3, inc-kw) 6 times (30)
Row 8: purl
Row 9: knit
Row 10: purl
Row 11: (k3, k2tog) 6 times (24)
Row 12: purl
Row 13: (k2, k2tog) 6 times (18)
Row 14: purl
Row 15: (k1, k2tog) 6 times (12)
Row 16: purl
Row 17: (k2tog) 6 times (6)

Break off yarn leaving a long end and transfer to a stitch holder.

Body

Starting at the base of the body, cast on 6 st in MAIN

Row 1: (inc-kw) 6 times (12)
Row 2: purl
Row 3: (k1, inc-kw) 6 times (18)
Row 4: purl
Row 5: (k2, inc-kw) 6 times (24)
Row 6-30: continue in stst, starting and ending with a purl row
Row 31: (k2, k2tog) 6 times (18)
Row 32: purl
Row 33: (k1, k2tog) 6 times (12)
Row 34: purl
Row 35: (k2tog) 6 times (6)

Break off yarn leaving a long end and transfer stitches to a stitch holder.

Arms (make 2)

Using 3mm double-ended needles and leaving a long end, cast on 3 st using PINK and work i-cord as follows

Row 1: k3
Row 2: without turning the work, move the stitches to the other end of the needle, pass the wool round the back of the work. Keeping yarn tight, k3
Repeat row 2 until the arm measures 85mm.

Break off yarn leaving a long end, and transfer stitches to a stitch holder.

Legs (make 2)

Using 3mm double-ended needles and leaving a long end, cast on 4 st using PINK and work i-cord as follows

Row 1: k4
Row 2: without turning the work, move the stitches to the other end of the needle, pass the wool round the back of the work. Keeping yarn tight, k4
Repeat row 2 until the leg measures 95mm.

Break off yarn leaving a long end, and transfer stitches to a stitch holder

Wings (make 2)

starting at the base of the wing, cast on 3st using WHITE

Row 1: knit
Row 2: inc-kw, k1, inc-kw (5)
Row 3: inc-kw, k3, inc-kw (7)
Row 4: inc-kw, k6 (8)
Row 5: knit
Row 6: knit
Row 7: k2tog, k6 (7)
Row 8: k5, k2tog (6)
Row 9: k2tog, k4 (5)
Row 10: knit
Row 11: knit

Row 12: knit
Row 13: inc-kw, k4 (6)
Row 14: k5, inc-kw (7)
Row 15: inc-kw, k6 (8)
Row 16: k7, inc-kw (9)
Row 17: inc-kw, k8 (10)
Row 18: k9, inc-kw (11)
Row 19: knit
Row 20: knit
Row 21: knit
Row 22: k2tog, k7, k2tog (9)
Row 23: k2tog, k5, k2tog (7)
Row 24: k2tog, k3, k2tog (5)
Row 25: k2tog, k1, k2tog (3)
Row 26: cast-off kw

Break yarn leaving a long end.

Skirt

Using MAIN and 3mm needles, cast on 60 st

Rows 1-30: knit
Cast-off kw.

Curls (make 10)

Using hair colour and 3mm needles cast on 30 st

Row 1: cast-off tightly kw.

To make up

Head

Fit the safety eyes roughly in the middle of the head, and close together. Thread the yarn from the last row of the head through the stitches remaining on the needle and pull tight, then remove the stitches from the needle. With right-sides together, sew along the back of the head, leaving a small gap at the base for stuffing. Turn the head the right way out, and stuff to the required firmness. Sew together the remaining opening and feed the end of the yarn back through the head before cutting off. Feed the remaining end back through the head before cutting off.

Body

Thread the yarn from the last row of the body through the stitches remaining on the needle and pull tight, then remove the stitches from the needle. With right-sides together, sew along the back of the body, leaving a small gap at the bottom for stuffing. Turn the body the right way out, and stuff to the required firmness. Sew together the remaining opening and feed the end of the yarn back through the body before cutting off. Feed the remaining end back through the body before cutting off.

Arms

Thread the yarn from the last row of the arm through the stitches remaining on the needle and pull tight, then remove the stitches from the needle. Fasten off this end securely. Weave the other loose end up through the arm and cut off the excess.

Legs

Thread the yarn from the last row of the leg through the stitches remaining on the needle and pull tight, then remove the stitches from the needle. Fasten off this end securely. Weave the other loose end up through the leg and cut off the excess.

Skirt

Bring short ends together to form a loop making sure the work is not twisted and sew along the short edge.

Assembly:

Attach the head to the body, making sure the eyes point forward (the body seam should be at the back).

Using the free thread, attach the arms to the body just below the head, one on each side.

Using the free thread, attach the legs to the underside of the body.

Using small running stitch, thread a piece of yarn around the top of the skirt loop, and gather the skirt around the body of the fairy, approximately half way down the body. Sew to the body and weave in any loose ends.

Sew the wings to the rear of the body as shown in the picture.

Attach the curls to the head, working on alternate sides. Weave in any loose ends. Give the curls a quick twist if they are looking too straight.

Rodney the Reindeer

Materials.

To make Rodney you will need the following:

DK wool in red

DK wool in brown

2 x 6mm safety eyes

stuffing

3mm knitting needles

3mm double ended needles

embroidery needle

Head

Starting at the nose and leaving a long end, cast on 3 st using RED

Row 1: (inc-kw) 3 times (6)
Row 2: purl
Row 3: (inc-kw) 6 times (12)
Row 4: purl
Row 5: change to BROWN, (inc-kw, k2, inc-kw) 3 times (18)
Row 6: purl
Row 7: k5, inc-kw, k6, inc-kw, k5 (20)
Row 8: purl
Row 9: k6, inc-kw, k6, inc-kw, k6 (22)
Row 10: purl
Row 11: k7, inc-kw, k6, inc-kw, k7 (24)
Row 12: purl
Row 13: k8, inc-kw, k6, inc-kw, k8 (26)
Row 14: purl
Row 15: k9, inc-kw, k6, inc-kw, k9 (28)
Row 16: purl
Row 17: k9, k2tog, k6, k2tog, k9 (26)
Row 18: p8, p2tog, p6, p2tog, p8 (24)
Row 19: k7, k2tog, k6, k2tog, k7 (22)

Row 20: purl
Row 21: (k2tog) 11 times (11)
Row 22: (p2tog twice), p3, (p2tog) twice (7)

Break yarn leaving a long end for sewing up the head, and place the stitches on a stitch holder.

Body

Starting at the base of the body cast on 6 st in BROWN

Row 1: (inc-kw) 6 times (12)
Row 2: purl
Row 3: (k1, inc-kw) 6 times (18)
Row 4: purl
Row 5: (k2, inc-kw) 6 times (24)
Row 6: purl
Row 7: k10, inc-kw, k2, inc-kw, k10 (26)
Row 8: p10, inc-pw, p1, inc-pw twice, p1, inc-pw, p10 (30)
Row 9: k10, inc-kw, k1, inc-kw, k4, inc-kw, k1, inc-kw, k10 (34)
Row 10: purl
Row 11: knit
Row 12: purl
Row 13: k10, k2tog, k1, k2tog, k4, k2tog, k1, k2tog, k10 (30)
Row 14: p10, p2tog, p1, p2tog twice, p1, p2tog, p10 (26)
Row 15: k10, k2tog, k2, k2tog, k10 (24)
Row 16-24: starting and ending with a purl row, continue in stst.
Row 25: (k2, k2tog) 6 times (18)
Row 26: purl
Row 27: (k1, k2tog) 6 times (12)
Row 28: purl
Row 29: (k2tog) 6 times (6)

Break off yarn leaving a long end to sew up body, and transfer stitches to a stitch holder.

Arms (make 2)

Using 3mm double-ended needles and leaving a long end, cast on 3 st using BROWN and work i-cord as follows

Row 1: k3
Row 2: without turning the work, move the stitches to the other end of the needle, pass the wool round the back of the work. Keeping yarn tight, k3

Repeat row 2 until the arm measures 85mm.

Break off yarn leaving a long end, and transfer stitches to a stitch holder

Legs (make 2)

Using 3mm double-ended needles and leaving a long end, cast on 4 st using BROWN and work i-cord as follows

Row 1: k4
Row 2: without turning the work, move the stitches to the other end of the needle, pass the wool round the back of the work. Keeping yarn tight, k4
Repeat row 2 until the arm measures 95mm.

Break off yarn leaving a long end, and transfer stitches to a stitch holder.

Antlers (make 2)

Using 3mm double-ended needles and leaving a long end, cast on 4 st using BROWN and work i-cord as follows

Row 1: k4
Row 2: without turning the work, move the stitches to the other end of the needle, pass the wool round the back of the work. Keeping yarn tight, k4

Repeat row 2 until the antler measures 24mm.

Branch

Row 1: k2, then put the remaining 2 st on a stitch holder.

Continue in i-cord on these 2 stiches for 3 rows.
Cast off kw. Break off yarn.

Re-join yarn and work i-cord on the last 2 stitches for 6 rows.
Cast-off kw. Break off yarn.

Tail

Starting at the base of the tail and leaving a long end, cast on 4 st in BROWN.

Row 1: (inc-kw) 4 times (8)
Row 2: knit
Row 3: inc-kw, k1, inc-kw, k2, inc-kw, k1, inc-kw (12)
Row 4: knit
Row 5: inc-kw, k1, inc-kw, k1, inc-kw, k2, inc-kw, k1, inc-kw, k1, inc-kw (18)
Row 6: knit
Row 7: (k2tog, k1) twice, k2tog, k2, k2tog, (k1, k2tog) twice (12)
Row 8: knit
Row 9: (k2tog) 6 times (6)

Row 10: knit
Row 11: (k2tog) 3 times (3)

Break off yarn leaving a long end and transfer stitches to a stitch holder.

Ears (make 2)

Cast on 6 st using BROWN

Row 1-3: knit
Row 4: k2tog, k2, k2tog (4)
Row 5: (k2tog) twice (2)
Row 6: k2tog (1)
Row 7:Cast off kw.

To make up

Head

Fit the safety eyes roughly a third of the way along the head from the nose, and roughly a quarter of the way in from each side. Thread the yarn from the last row of the head through the stitches remaining on the needle and pull tight, then remove the stitches from the needle. With right-sides together, sew along the base of the head, leaving a small gap at the nose for stuffing.
Turn the head the right way out, and stuff to the required firmness. Sew together the remaining opening and feed the end of the yarn back through the head before cutting off. Feed the remaining end back through the head before cutting off.

Body

Thread the yarn from the last row of the body through the stitches remaining on the needle and pull tight, then remove the stitches from the needle. With right-sides together, sew along the back of the body, leaving a small gap at the bottom for stuffing. Turn the body the right way out, and stuff to the required firmness. Sew together the remaining opening and feed the end of the yarn back through the body before cutting off. Feed the remaining end back through the body before cutting off.

Arms

Thread the yarn from the last row of the arm through the stitches remaining on the needle and pull tight, then remove the stitches from the needle. Fasten off this end securely. Weave the other loose end up through the arm and cut off the excess.

Legs

Thread the yarn from the last row of the leg through the stitches remaining on the needle and pull tight, then remove the stitches from the needle. Fasten off this end securely. Weave the other loose end up through the leg and cut off the excess.

Ears

Thread the yarn from the last row of the ear through the side of the ear before cutting off. Fold the ear in half length-wise and join across the bottom.

Tail

Thread the yarn from the last row of the tail through the stitches remaining on the needle and pull tight, then remove the stitches from the needle. Fold the tail in half lengthwise and sew along the edge leaving an opening at the bottom. Turn the tail inside out and stuff lightly. Sew up the opening and fasten off the yarn securely. Thread the end back through the tail before cutting off.

Antlers

Thread the yarn from the last row of each branch back through the antler and cut. Fasten off the threads at the base of each branch, and then feed the ends up the antler before trimming.

Assembly:

Attach the head to the body, making sure the nose points in the same direction as the stomach of the deer (the body seam should be at the back)

Using the free thread, attach the arms to the body just below the head, one on each side.

Using the free thread, attach the legs to the underside of the body.

Using the free end, attach the ears to the rear of the head, one on either side as in the pictures.

Using the free end, sew each antler to the top of the head between the ears, making sure the short branches face in opposite directions or forward.

Using the free thread, attach the tail to the rear of the body near the bottom, with the point facing upwards.

Lightning Source UK Ltd.
Milton Keynes UK
UKOW07f1342201117
313036UK00006B/168/P